Words Unspoken: Volume 1

Deeper Than Eyes Can See

Poetry by Tymeka Coney

authorHOUSE®

AuthorHouse™
1663 Liberty Drive
Bloomington, IN 47403
www.authorhouse.com
Phone: 1-800-839-8640

First published by AuthorHouse   10/07/2011

ISBN: 978-1-4634-2024-6 (sc)
ISBN: 978-1-4634-2023-9 (ebk)

Library of Congress Control Number: 2011910639

Printed in the United States of America

This book is printed on acid-free paper.

Book Design by Tymeka Coney
Cover design by Tymeka Coney & John Ferenz
Cover photographs and About the Author photograph by Dexter Browne Photography

For Booking or Contact:
1-877-37-WORDS
1-877-37(96737)
Email:WordsunspokenTymeka@yahoo.com
To Write:
Maka T Publishing /Meek Entertainment
P.O. Box 381133
Hollywood, California 90038
For Author Updates: www.tymekaconey.com
Follow TymekaConey on Twitter, Facebook and Myspace

Illustrations by
Bob Sunday
www.myspace.com/BobSunday
Smogcutter@yahoo.com
The Photos—21 pictures All original Art Work Featured Was Provided by Bob Sunday
own photo 22 Michael Jackson
own photo 23 President Barack Obama
own photo 24 Africa Flag
own photo 25 Hollywood Sign
own photo 26 Yolanda King and Tymeka Coney

"Words we feel, Words that heal, Words that appeal to our five senses of touch, smell, see, hear, taste. Words from the past, Words for the future, Words from my heart and soul, mind, body and spirit to you and yours."

Tymeka Coney

Contents

III. The Past

IV. The Future

V. Feeling

VI. My Heart, Soul and Mind

VII. Haiku

Introduction/Acknowledgments

Giving praises to God from whom all blessings flow! I thank you for all the gifts you've given me. "Every good and perfect gift comes from above."—James 1:17 One of my mentors Tyler Perry who has managed to succeed as a multi-hyphenate once quoted, "A man's gift makes room for him and brings him before great men." Proverbs 18:16 I get excited about that scripture. I am thankful to my Heavenly Father that we have a relationship and I am able to know the wisdom of you and your "Words Unspoken", and Spoken to me and that I now lead a "Purpose-Driven Life.""Words Unspoken," are all the words that I want to say from my mind, body and spirit, but I don't often express them verbally. Now I share them with you by writing them and expressing them poetically. Given the fact that they are heartfelt . . . . I am sure that as you are reading "Words Unspoken", you will find one poem out of many that will speak to you.

I thank you, Mom, Joann Coney, and Dad, Lemo Coney II, for the gift of life.

Thank you, Mom, for your prayers and constant wisdom and support, personally and professionally. I appreciate you for not accepting less than I am capable of in working towards my goals and for loving me enough to "Keep it Real," with me. These words merely express my gratitude and love for you. Thanks Dad for instilling discipline in me at an early age. It has been instrumental in shaping me to be the woman that I am today.

Thanks to my brother, Lemo Coney III, for the inspiration and advice you give through your gifts and for the partnership/strength to endure all that we've experienced through our *Common Bond* in Texas and California. Keep singing and writing and performing too! We are in this together boo!! I love you!!!!

To my two Grandmas;

"Momma" Clara Coney- Thank you for your prayers and encouragement in all that I do and for keeping me active in church as a young girl.

Jerlene "Jewel" Sims—Thanks for your undying love and support and for your prayers and for taking me to work with you at a young age, helping me to realize the value of work in my early and later years!!

To my two Grandpas, Henry Cooper and Elmo Coney-Thank you for your entrepreneurship and hard work. Your legacy lives on through me and I feel you smiling down from Heaven.

Thanks again to my boy, Bob Sunday, for your artistic contributions. Thanks for the homegrown love and continued success to you in your artistic endeavors.

Shout out to hip-hop artist "Dirty" for believing in my lyrical gift and giving me a place to record my spoken word.

Thank you to Tammi Mac, On-Air Personality KJLH102.3 FM Radio, Los Angeles, for your support of my talents.

Thanks to John "Xeno Cyd" Ferenz and Kennard Reed for all of your assistance with constant computer work needed to complete the process of getting the book done.

Again, to all of my friends and family who I could not mention—you should know who you are! Love to all of you and thank you for your support!!

To the nay-sayers . . . well, I care not mention.

Everything, whether negative or positive, has all worked for me. My favorite scripture is "And we know all things work together for the good of those who love him and are called according to his purpose."—Romans 8:28

To my English teachers and all of those with whom I've had a relationship—You never know how you've inspired me to write in some way. Thanks to Pastor Harlan and now Rev. Tommy L. Brown and the Ervay Cedar Missionary Baptist Church Family in Dallas, Texas, where I was active growing up and who helped shape my writing and oratorical gifts as a youth.

To the second church I attended, where I was spiritually fed and creatively inspired through the words and accomplishments of Bishop T.D. Jakes at The Potter's House in Dallas, Texas, and to my current church of 9 years, The City of Refuge Church in Gardena, California, where I have had the honor to serve as the Drama Ministry Director for 2 years, and to my Spiritual Father, Bishop Noel Jones, for his constant reminder through his illustrious sermons about our gifts.

"To one, he gave one talent. To some, he gave more than one talent."—Matthew 25:15 "Our gifts/callings are God's gift to us and what we do with those gifts is our gift to him." Thank you to Pastor Sarah Morgan and the Women of Vision/Vision International Ministries family. Thank you Pastor Sarah Morgan for all of the powerful words you've spoken in my life and over my life . . . When you shared with me "that I am a scribe," you further confirmed that I must continue the work that God has begun in me.

Thank you to my spiritual sisters Pastor Althea Sims, Dr. Holly Davis-Carter, and Robi Reed and the Ascend Bible Study family who once a month give me that additional spiritual/ creative boost and encouragement through fellowship and the word to continue on the journey in Hollywood and Thank you to Dr. Holly Davis-Carter and Robi Reed for The Merge Summit that has inspired me for the last 3 years.

To all of my sorors of Delta Sigma Theta Sorority, Incorporated, worldwide, and to the Eta Lambda Chapter of Texas Tech University for your support.

I write from within. I express because it's therapeutic. My alter ego speaks up for me through poetry. I call her Tyme Lashae! I love creativity! I am mused and amused by creative individuals.

Art imitates life. Art is life! Art is poetry. I know my soulmate is an artist! Acting, Dancing, Singing, Writing, Painting and Reciting are all art forms of creativity. We all have a gift, and our purpose is to find that gift and share it with others. We all have that thing we would do for free in life. That's true passion.

In the words of the Great Poet Shakespeare, "To Thine Own Self Be True." I salute all the poets before me and present with me and those that shall come after me.

* **Poetry Featured in Rolling Out Magazine and Melt Magazine, 2006**
* **Sugar Honey Ice Tea from Upcoming Spoken Word Album**
* **Bonus Poems: Purpose-Driven Life, Ode to Oprah, A Tribute to the King "Gone Too Soon," A Salute to Phenomenal Women, Recession Proof**

Dedication page

I dedicate this book to my family and friends,

and to the loving memory of Dr. Martin Luther King Jr.'s oldest daughter, Ms. Yolanda Denise King, who passed away before I finished printing my book. She loved and wrote/recited poetry herself. I had the pleasure of meeting this beautiful angel along life's path and she enjoyed reading my poetry and believed in my talent. She was certainly poetic in the way she carried herself and spoke. Most importantly was the way she continued to carry out her father's dream. She told me, "Keep your eyes on your prize" "Stay strong and keep God first and You will see all of your dreams come true," and "I hope that one day we will work together." Today, we work together in spirit!! Your memories and dreams live on, Dr. Martin Luther King Jr., Mrs. Coretta Scott King, and last, but not least, my friend and one of my mentors, Ms. Yolanda Denise King. 5/15/07
Rest in Peace. "YOKI."

I. HEALING

Spring

April showers bring May flowers right after March.
Overcast in the sky, as kids
wave goodbye and take a break for a week.
Go down to the creek and throw rocks.
Roll down the street listening to hip hop.
At the beach, running in the sand.
Scuba diving, surviving the heat with sunblock while you tan.
Females rollerblading, walking their dogs,
Men driving fancy cars, while others play volleyball.
I love the gentle breeze that blows your hair,
Free in the wind, relaxing without care.
Spring—an introduction to Summer,
Reminding us how important it is to work out and get fit.
Spring—reminding you to Spring back and Spring forward and don't quit,
and if there are some things leftover from Winter,
Why not do some Spring cleaning,
and give life new meaning.
Spring—What a wonderful part of the four seasons.

Shades of You

Feeling blue
Green with envy
Steamy hot red light in bed
Room for gray clouds of confusion
when its either black or white
Not in between the golden touch of your hand
Sandy brown
hair that sat next to me on a couch of burgundy
Remembered my favorite color was turquoise
Yellows and pinks
seemed to standout
but no purple of royalty
or loyalty
Sea green feels deep
yet silver outshines the secrecy
as we uncover several colors of mystery
I only see "Misty Blue"
When I visualize
Shades of you.

Sunshine and Rain

Sometimes you grow tired of pain
Going through things over and over again
Want to smile again
Need sunshine for the rain
You want to be happy and move dark clouds away
In hopes of a better day
Storm clouds push to get in your way
Darkness clouds you with feelings of gray
and feeling sad and blue
want to go back to doing the things
you're used to—but interrupted
Ready to resume but no clue
Rain puddles fall from a face that
is tired of pain and anguish
Waiting on colors of a rainbow
and colors of yellow
Waiting on sunshine for rain
and a chance to smile again

Life . . . Another Opportunity

Sometimes funny . . . don't understand
How we end up
Where we end
But it all appears
To be a part of his divine plan
Don't often comprehend the road map
Or the directions to take
But
Acknowledging him as he directs
Our paths is the road I take
Everyday I awake
I'm thanking God for
A brand new day
And sending
New opportunities my way

Please Help Me!

I'm out here in the cold trying to make it before I get too old
Folks hating standing in my way
While I get on my knees and pray before I say what I should not say
Don't understand silly games people play
All I try to do is find my way
Through to my destination with no hesitation
No more obstacles, simply opportunities
Open the door and I'll get it myself
Yet you don't want to help me, just hurt me
While I keep asking
Please Help Me!
Lend a helping hand when you see me doing the best I can
Until then I'll just stand when I've done all I can
So again I'm back
What happened
to if I scratch your back and you scratch mine?
Or instead of trying to kill me softly, kill me with kindness
It's true he helps those that help themselves, so
I just look to the hills from which cometh my help
Lord Please Help Me!

Music

Music to me is melodies from the heart.
Music in its greatest form is a work of art.
Not only is music my favorite past time, but it's a way I communicate my feelings.
When I'm feeling down, it is also used for my healing.
Music is definitely a gift from God, and appeals to anyone who listens.
When you're mad it can also release tension.
If it weren't for Music, where would we be?
There is so much to appreciate from the blues all the way down to the symphony.
Music as it does appeal to all and definitely relates.
It should be highly respected and used.
If you haven't listened, hurry up before it's too late.
Don't abuse it. Refuse it. But use it.
You've got to love it.
Music.

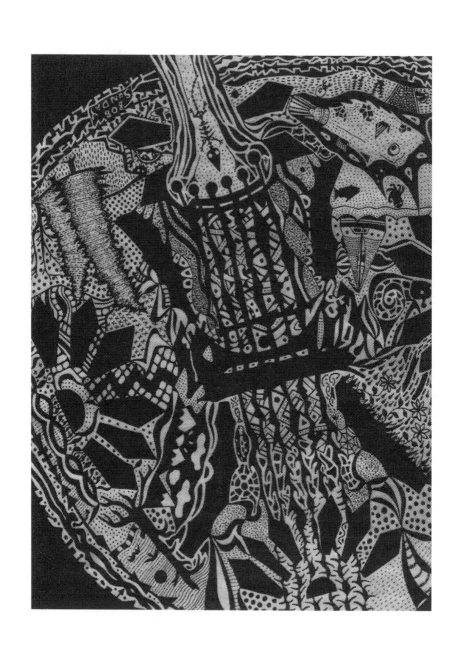

Chillin' Bobbin' to the Music

As I sit here amongst the crowd of my people
I can't help but observe the way we feel
the way we groove
Chillin' Bobbin' to the music
As I sit here in the room
I'm in awe because of the appreciation
I feel the deep inspiration
I feel for the way the music heals and thrills your inner soul
Sit back, relax, as the music takes control
I don't know maybe it's the Rap, R&B or just the beats
that make my people feel so free
As I listen and smile and watch my friends bounce in the corner
I feel the dance,the communication through the mind to the ear from the
ear to the mouth
From the East Coast, West Coast the North and Down South
Chillin' Bobbin' to the music
A legend that lives on through every generation, every song
What started out as something to pass the time
as the Underground Railroad increased to decline
now has developed into sight to the blind and education for the mind
I hope you understand our leisure
Don't mistake it for your pleasure
A gift from the Creator keeps getting greater and greater
Love through music reaches to the hearts of all who don't refuse it
It will set your mind at ease and your conscious mind free
It all happened while
We were
I was
You will be
Chillin' Bobbin' to the music.

Cloudy

Sunlight in two sunsets
Calm wind blowing
With a thunderstorm, rains raindrops
Tastes as sweet as lollipops
Curves of Grand Canyon
Deep as the Bermuda Triangle
Great as The Michigan Lake
Touch the valley low
While in the Sahara Desert
Taken to the mountaintop
Of the wettest Amazon River
An Erie Canal never seen in the tunnel of love
Yet the perfect weather for two-getherness
Forecast of hail ahead
Yet laying on a bed of roses
A rainbow keeps storm clouds away
Let's escape to the oceans and seas of eternity.

Forest for the Trees

Sometimes in life we can't see the forest for the trees
and we don't quite understand the birds and the bees
and life's struggles cause us to fall to our knees and pray
even when we don't know the right words to say
We want to change but we don't know how
We want to rid the past and live in the now
But the memories have left an indelible print in our mind that make it hard
to get to the other side
We've got some positives and negatives
Feelings of being neglected, rejected, subjected to trees
with no roots and no fruits and barking up the wrong trees
Sometimes we've suppressed pain
We wanted to let go
Suggested rain and didn't wait for the rainbow
Depressed, oppressed in need of light and the will to do right
But wrong is all you know
Trying to make it through the Forest, yet there's so many trees
Sent a Forest ranger in the form of an Angel
Yet a stranger that could be danger.
But how do you know?
So what do you do?
Trying to make it through the Forest
Need help but try to ignore it before it overshadows you.
Sometimes you have to trust what you don't see
Walk by faith and know that thou art with thee and the rod and staff shall
comfort thee as you walk through the valley
when you've never taken this particular journey
As you move each tree the next will lead you to a closer destiny
Sometimes it's not evident on the surface
Sometimes you have to wander in the Forest to go deep
After all, the Forest wouldn't be a Forest without the company of trees and
a Forest couldn't be a Forest without the Creator almighty.
With him you'll make it out no doubt.
You'll see the Forest for the trees.

Deeper Than Eyes Can See

Surfaces that reach
but oceans go deeper than
eyes can see
In the valley
reaching valley lows
But starting to climb mountain peaks
Waves flowing as currents
while currently feeling
the heat
Heat wave of energy from
eyes that meet
and the rhythm in sync
with every beat of every measure
temperatures that rise and fall
like underlined pressure
on the barometer, thermostat
adjusted to cater to every need
Yet the need to go deeper
Somehow leads to beyond the sea
see windows of the soul tell
enough for all seasons
why it's cold, hot, but never quite
understanding the reasons
Maybe one day what lies beneath
as roots under a tree
will soon come to
the top after digging deep
to the bottom
Soon we will change disbelief to
something well achieved
Uncovering everything underneath
Covering the mind, body and spirit 3 in 1 and 1 in 3
Deeper than mere eyes can see

God I Know You Hear Me

God I know you hear me out there
and I know you care
I know you are always there
to hear my prayers
Lately I've been going through
things I don't quite understand
and I'm reaching
but I don't feel your hand
I've been trying to do the best I can
in every area of my life
Yet I still end up going while growing
through trials in life and people with strife
I know you came that we might have life
abundantly
Yet I feel I'm living sometimes beneath
God I know you hear me
Grant me the serenity
to conquer the enemy so that I might have liberty
to know I can have all things that I ask in your name
and that you hear me every time I call your name

Stability

Tired of living life like this
I wish I could control these issues
Literally and gain some stability through this humility
leaving me with no sensibility as I am
placed on the hit list from the enemy
Every time I rise I fall
Got a phone can't receive phone calls
Got rent paid, but no more till pay day
Can't call on one friend when things aren't going your way
What do you do when all the hustle is hustled out of you?
Saying forgive them for they know not what they do,
but like a tree planted by the water, I shall not be moved
Want to smile and laugh to keep from crying
Want to continue with life, but you feel like dying
Got dreams and goals, but what's the use in trying
Praying for God to hear you and take all the pain away
They say more money, more problems
But no money, more problems
They say if life gives you lemons, make lemonade
What if there's no lemons and life's left you bittersweet?
Saying God please help me get back on my feet
Keep this spiritual and physical food in me when I'm hungry and need to
eat
God grant me the serenity, tranquility, through all the humility but most
of all
Give me STABILITY!

Laugh out Loud—LOL

Laughter is the best medicine
It's so much easier to smile than frown
Laugh out Loud-LOL
It cheers you up
It connects you
It relaxes you
Laugh out Loud-LOL
When you're feeling down
I write this poem
to lift you from your depression
to add laughter to your life
Laugh out Loud-LOL
Think happy thoughts
Celebrate the kid in you as you kid around
Laugh out Loud-LOL
Laugh at the clown with the red nose
Laugh at the stand-up comedian telling jokes
Laugh out Loud-LOL
Watching sitcoms or simply having fun
With no pun intended
It turns enemies to friends
It turns negatives to positives
Laugh out Loud-LOL
Sad days to happy days
Text it—LOL
Spread it across the airwaves
When you are sick or feeling blue
I offer this remedy to you
Laugh out Loud-LOL
Laughter is the best medicine
It's so much easier to smile than frown
Laugh out Loud-LOL

II. APPEALING

Candy

Sweet as honey dew
But vicious as voodoo
Words that soothe the intellect
Words that stimulate regret
Sweet Candy
Comes in handy for the sweet tooth
Causes cavity
by the gravity
that takes a hold on you
Sweet
I wish it wasn't bad
for me causing sugar diabetes
internally
Always need some for now and later
Comes in handy
I call it Candy.

Your Lady

Love me
Hold me
Cherish me
I am your lady
Take me out
Hold my hand
Let me know you understand
Promise me you're my man
I am your lady
Don't tell me lies
Sing me lullabies
Tonight no thighs
But maybe a kiss goodbye
I am your lady.

I am a Lady
Featured in Melt Magazine

In my femininity, in my virginity
In my tranquility, in my serenity
I am a lady
In my mystery, and in my privacy
I am a lady
In my confidence, in my arrogance
In my humbleness, in my opulence
I am a lady
In my boldness, in my coldness
In the sway of my hips, in the lick of my lips
I am a lady
In my intelligence, in my innocence
I am a lady
In my quietness, in my shyness
I am a lady
In my beauty, in my nudity
I am a lady
Don't try to sway me, persuade me, betray me, portray me
But embrace me, appreciate me.
Although I'm not like every one
I'm one in a million,
"Once, Twice, Three Times a Lady."
Not the "Lady and the Tramp" or "The Lady That Sings the Blues"
More like the first lady to you!
Capital L-A-D-Y
I AM A LADY!!!!

Mr. Debonair

A debonair man with class and style,
Make a woman go crazy, make a woman go wild.
A debonair man with a plan in his hand,
Make a woman go ballistic and for him she'll stand.
It's not all about the muscles or the sweat that glistens down his spine.
But it's undoubtedly the intelligence and courage that stimulates his mind,
My mind or your mind.
This man is making moves to the music he grooves
You feel him, you see him
Like blind but now you see.
A man with D-E-B-O-N-A-I-R, Debonair written all over his body.
Some like them short, some like them tall.
Some like them dark, some like them light.
But I can assure you that whatever the case,
He is represented day and night.
Swim wear, Casual wear, Formal wear, Sleep wear, Under wear, Any where
Ladies do we care?
Blue Collar, Man of the Cloth, Entertainer, Business Man, Entrepreneur,
Six Figures, Sports Figure, Goal-Oriented or Billionaire,
Just as long as he's got talent and work he does his share.
Fellows don't hate.
Ladies I know you can't wait.
Get off your derriere and
Embrace Mr. Debonair.

Chills Down My Spine
(I Ain't Even Lyin')

You see when I see you walking by with that smile and those sexy lips
Reminds me of the taste of honey
No honey dip
Is it the way you walk?
Is it the way you talk?
Is it that deep build or that skin so soft and smell so fresh?
No it must be those jeans
Umm . . . now let me guess?
You know you are too fine
With these
Chills Down My Spine
I Ain't Even Lyin'.
Got me thinking of the time
When love was blind
Am I losing my mind?
Ooh . . . .
these Chills Down My Spine.
I Ain't Even Lyin'.
This feels so divine.
You've got to be mine
This love is real
Not just some line
With these
Chills Down My Spine
I Ain't Even Lyin'.

Forbidden Fruit

Sexy, cute
Thinking of all the things I could do to you
Touch you
Hold you
Taste you
Juices flowing
Mind blowing
Peachy keen
Never seen
But you know what I mean
Sweet nectar
In every sector
Of your being
Fresh ripened
Peel by peel
Sending chills down my spine to the vine
Of every grind
Smells of passion fruit linger in my nose
As I'm tempted to bite off more than I can chew
I've already stepped into the garden
Started to see fruition from a planted seed
I've got to get this fruit while it's in season
Pricey
But the right pick for me
I'll deal with the consequences later.

Like a Virgin

Touched for the very first time and intertwined
wanted to wine and dine but that takes time
to get to know before you flow to the
Delta down low
Want to spread it like jelly
and make it smelly
But it's tight like a jar of hair grease
like dax you want to wax free and
melt it down
but it's tight like glue and it don't get sticky and it won't mildew
It's not hot but it's got chills it sends you through
As you try to divide and conquer your hunger
A salivating dog in heat
But thighs stay closed
And eyes wide shut
And open wide don't meet

What Voo Did You Do?

What voo did you do to me?
Got me under this spell although I can't quite
Put it in words
Thinking of you everyday
Wanting thoughts to vanish away
Deep thoughts that prayers can't shake
Or get the mountains to move
Me out of these valley lows
I want to know
I've got to know
What voo did you do to me?
Superstitions of intuitions
About the way I feel for you
No matter what you do
I still end up loving you
A hex to get next to me
Under my skin while you send
Me on a wild goose chase
For your love
Was it blood that became
Thicker than the love shared between us two?
Wanted my t-shirt to sleep with
Yet I'm reminded of you
Please answer this question
What voo did you do?

Sugar Honey Ice Tea

Sugar Honey Ice Tea is featured from the
Upcoming Spoken Word Album
To listen to Sugar Honey Ice Tea performed by Tymeka
Coney
Go to: http://www.myspace.com/tymelashaepoetry

Sugar Honey Ice Tea

Sweet as Sugar
Brown and smooth as Honey
Cool As Ice
Good to you like money green tea.
Sugar Honey Ice Tea
When you talking to me makes me believe we were meant to be
Don't even have to pinch me
It's not a dream
It's what it seems
Can't believe how we connect so quickly and honestly
I can't forget thee
the feel I get completely as you effect me totally
Mentally, Physically and Spiritually
Sugar Honey Ice Tea
Is what I feel every time I'm in your presence
Acquiescing this blessing flowing upon me.
Got me praying to keep from saying
Sugar Honey Ice Tea
And praying on my knees asking begging please forgive me
and prevent me from doing things unpleasing
Because the proclitude gives me the intestinal fortitude
to act upon my proclivities
But it's simple
Our bodies are a temple and though I'm tempted
I'm just preempted to take a sip
Sugar Honey Ice Tea
Soothing, smoothing, eluding to the aroma
That lets me know it's good Karma
That we met
and I ain't even had one cup yet
Sugar Honey Ice Tea
Flows and flows and
Sprinkles of sweetness
Flows and flows
of sticky substance from the nectar of a beautiful flower
Flows and flows of

Frozen water that chills me
and send chills down my spine and then the meltdown in boiling water
Make you want to quench the spirit as you quench your thirst
But you resort back to the verse before you
become immersed and your feelings get hurt
Sugar Honey Ice Tea
I feel like I'm the Sugar Honey Ice Tea
Being with you feels like Sugar Honey Ice Tea
My senses don't seem to make sense
Because its blowing my mind with every grind
of Sugar Honey Ice Tea
I smell the Sugar Honey Ice Tea
I touch the Sugar Honey Ice Tea
I taste the Sugar Honey Ice Tea
I feel the Sugar Honey Ice Tea
I see the Sugar Honey Ice Tea
See I could warm up to you in the morning and cool down to you at night
just as long as you never leave my sight
Everything will be alright
I need sugar
you need honey
I got ice and you got tea
See I complement you—you complement me
Sugar Honey Ice Tea

III. THE PAST

Remembering You

Started a tradition of strong will.
Visited every hot summer because we had to.
However, the time spent we learned so much.
Never knowing that one day a lady that woke us up to black coffee and cream and stories untold,
A lady that taught us to make homemade donuts from powdered sugar and flaky biscuits made of dough,
Would soon vanish away like Winter that once had white snow.
How I waited to hear a soft-spoken voice call me "Little Sister."
Embrace me with warmth like a bear hug to a cub.
Taught me to stand on a stool and wash dishes at a young age.
Feels bad now cause you wanted me to eat all my vegetables, but I slipped them under the table to the salivating dog.
Never knowing as I was growing up, you were also growing old.
Until the day they had to put you in a nursing home.
For Alzheimer's disease became jealous and had taken control over our tradition, our relationship, and everything we once shared.
It just hurt so much to see all these strangers living with someone for whom I cared.
It's me, "Little Sister." Do you still remember me?
I was once catching lightning bugs, grasshoppers and walking down the dirt roads and drinking
RC cola from the corner stores as everyone passed by and waved at me.
As I taste the salt that runs down my face of bittersweet memories.
There's nothing left to do.
I wonder will I ever see you again, and will you remember me then.
I Remember You.

Independence Day

Declaration of Independence
July 4, 1976
Like hearing fireworks on the Fourth of July
I realize the holiday is nearby
As I see Independence Day approaching
I'm feeling something serious and I'm not joking.
I'm thinking, Yes we are free,
But what are we free from?
Is it the hatred, the beating, the killing, the racism, the starvation?
No, I don't think so!
We've got people locked up, dying and struggling to get off probation.
When you think of Independence,
What could this possibly mean to you?
Freedom from the past struggles, and a change for the better
Or just another day to get together and drink and eat barbecue.
It upsets me when I see my people who have ancestors that have fought hard
to get us to where we are today.
Then we don't do anything to aid in the continuation of this, instead we ask
for a day off work with pay.
All I am trying to get you to see and understand,
Is to be proud of how far we have come and stop blaming everything on
the man.
Instead of focusing on all the negatives,
Let's focus on the positives my people and whatever you believe in take a
stand.
After all, this is Independence Day!
Spread love, unity and peace.
We are free all across the land.

I Live in a Country

I live in a country where character and the heart no longer matter.
Instead people tend to judge you based on your status and how high you are
on the economic ladder.
I live in a country where character and the heart no long matter.
Instead they look at the color of your skin and it seems it gets worse
Considering if yours is much darker—better yet, blacker.
I live in a country where character and the heart no longer matter.
Instead they tried to impeach a leader of our country not because he did his
job, or because he balanced the budget
But what really matters?
I live in a country where character and the heart no longer matter.
Instead people discriminate, disintegrate, hate, don't congratulate, don't
motivate,
Don't educate, and don't demonstrate.
Yet they probate, fornicate, perpetrate and intimidate
Please, Please . . .
Let's seize the hate.
There's no time to wait.
Lest you don't intend to enter the gate.
I live in a country where character and the heart no longer matter.
When really if you take the time out and besides the outside,
View the entire package.
You will realize—
We live in a country where character and the heart indeed matter.

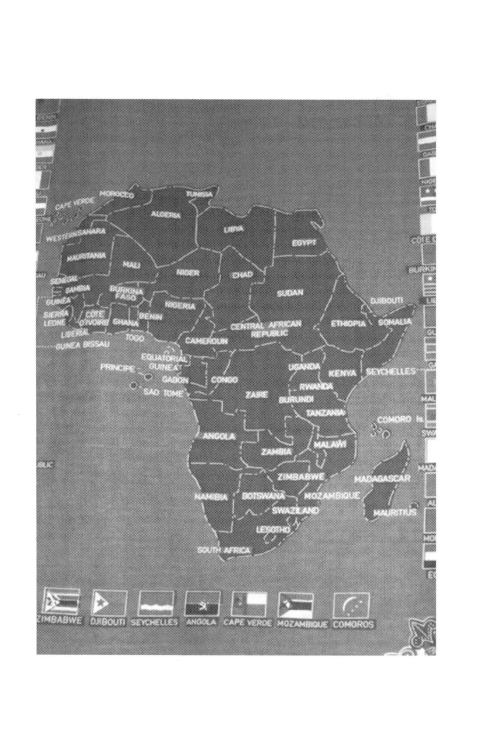

I Sing to Africa

I sing to Africa
To timbers, diamonds and gold and ancient stories untold
I sing to Africa
to my Kings
I sing to Africa
I am a Queen
I sing to Africa
"Lift Every Voice and Sing"
I sing to Africa
And run with the zebras, tigers, gazelles and lions
I sing to Africa
With drums and folk songs and my African dance
I sing to Africa
In the Motherland
I sing to Africa
From the Sahara Desert to the Safari and Swahili
I sing to Africa
To my ancestors, history makers and trailblazers
I sing to Africa
To Nelson Mandela's Freedom
I sing to Africa
To cure Aids, Malaria and starving children
I sing to Africa
Celebrating my African American existence because it's part of my heritage
I sing to Africa
Ethiopia, Ghana,Somalia, Nigeria, Zimbabwe, Sierra Leone, West to the
United States
I sing to Africa
Through Kwanzaa
I sing to Africa
To my royal Priesthood of Nubian Kings and Queens
I sing to Africa
To Thee I sing — Africa!

Freedom

Freedom—is defined as the quality or state of being free. Independence. Exemption.
Release or Ease. Facility. Frankness. Unrestricted. A political right or privilege.

Freedom

Well since I have freedom of speech and expression
I might as well teach and preach this lesson
a blessing through a sermon
some Freedom of religion for you to learn and discern
That there's a lot of things I have to say
Get off my chest
Freedom of the press
through the Freedom of this assembly
"Freedom" is liberty
Some Emancipation Proclamation for blind eyes to see
Don't mean to freeload on your generosity with animosity
but it's reciprocity that I give in the form of a freebie
I'm a free thinker intellectually
But I want to put it to you in the right way
There's so much going on and on and on in the world today
I don't understand how it all got this way
We need freedom to ring to see things clearer
and hold things dearer cause the end is getting nearer and nearer
If we've got freedom why are people getting shot for no reason
and we can't tell what the weather is and which season
Folks don't know who to believe in
Yet we all cry Freedom
Like Dr. Martin Luther King said "Let Freedom Ring"
Like Maya Angelou "Let the Caged bird Sing"
Freedom is what the constitution guarantees
Sometimes I just think Bill ain't right
I sometimes still don't feel free
Maybe it's me freestanding the freedman to erase the slave mentality
I want to be free, free to be me
Free to walk across the street without someone eying me
and trying to steal from me or sell to me
Freedom to wear what I want and to drive what I want to drive
Have a 9 to 5 or just freelance to get by
Freedom to stop those that freebase to get high and be
Free as a bird with wings
Free like "My Country 'Tis of Thee"
I salute the statue of liberty
I pledge of allegiance to colors of serenity
Red, blue, white
I stand up and fight for what's right
Like black power with Power from above
I hold my fist in the air
I give grace to the almighty
After all he died that we might be free.
Freedom!!!

Black History

Black History seems to be a mystery to those that don't see the color.

They don't recognize the past struggles that so many have marched and died for.

So they sit back and criticize and wait to see what's in store.

In store is a history that's marked with Harriet Tubman's courage as she led the Underground Railroad.

In store are the words and disappointment in *Uncle Tom's Cabin*, written by Harriet Beecher Stowe.

In store is the intelligence, entertainment, success of the poet Maya Angelou.

In store are "Dreams Deferred," written by Langston Hughes.

However, redefined and kept alive like the hope of Jesse Jackson.

If we could just all have a dream like Dr. Martin Luther King Jr.

Remember that we must do everything it takes, "By Any Means Necessary," in the words of Malcolm X.

Pick up after these greats not just having one month to celebrate for 28 days.

History is to teach and enrich the lives of others as we

Stick together and love one another because contrary to the color, these are our fathers, mothers, sisters, and brothers.

Black History.

If only we could learn and appreciate those that have made a lot of privileges be.

Like Madam CJ Walker, our 1st Black millionaire, and who could forget the lovely Oprah Winfrey, one of our first black billionaires,

who cares enough to share with the world

and our leader, the 44th President of the United States, Barack Obama

and Michelle Obama, our 1st lady, and their two beautiful girls

for taking a stand and providing a stimulus to lend a helping hand

reminding us "Yes We Can"

all come together in unity.

Then Black History would be American History, not just a faded memory.

IV. THE FUTURE

Materialistic

Materialistic is your name
When you claim none of that matters
It's matters of the heart you say
Then you say what matters is where I stay
I'd let you come in
if you were my friend
If you were my real friend,
You'd be there till the end
Even if you never make it in
Materialistic is your name
As you play this game of hide and seek
You seek to rob me financially
When you know you can't stand me
If I was broke you wouldn't
lend a dime to me
What does it matter
the car I drive, the clothes I wear,
who does my hair or what is my 9 to 5?
Love me for me
It's all the same
Until you change your name
I can't talk to you
You've gone ballistic
You make me sick
Materialistic!

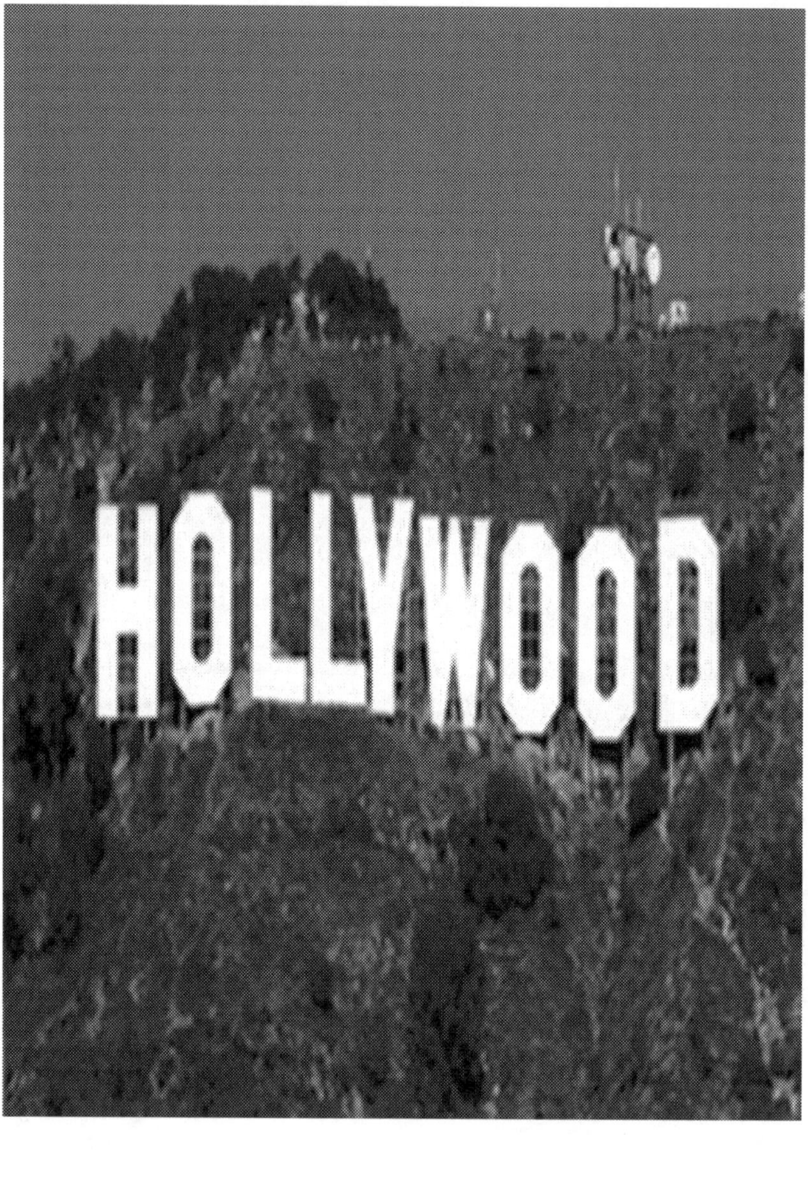
HOLLYWOOD

Hollywood

Where dreams really do come true.
Well, at least that's what they say.
It's crazy how I always dreamed I'd make it to this place one day.
I get here feeling like I can conquer the world.
Then my whole world gets turned upside down,
Where I'm feeling down from the roller coaster ride I've been on.
Yet I'm not going home.
I've got a mission I'm on.
You see there is a blank star left waiting on my name.
See I was born for this fame thing.
But they ain't recognizing I'm Hollywood.
They on some Hollywood issues!
It ain't about who I'm sleeping with,
What car I drive down Rodeo Drive.
It's what I have inside that keeps me alive.
When everyone is on that dope.
When they can't cope.
I'm keeping hope alive.
Can you believe Bob Hope died?
But he was in the game over 100 years and that's what I'm talking about.
Like the show *Cheers*, I'm at the place where everybody's going to know my
name.
I'm learning how to play this game.
I've got my own rules.
Yes, I live by the golden rules of what The Heavenly Father already promised
me—
That Hollywood was mine.
So . . . I'm just going to sit back while you count your dimes and
Wait on my time to shine—
Hollywood!!

You'll see

You should have called one day
Hopefully it won't be too late
For you to demonstrate
What you were simply trying to say
Yet you failed me
tried to get me to sell out
To some lies
I'm not buying from you
Like the real reason you do what you do
No one will ever be as good as I am
And have been and will always be
I'm real
I'm genuine, sincerely loving you
For eternity, exclusively
We were meant to be
Despite the enemy
Keeping you in disbelief
When you awake from make believe
Reality will set in
You'll see

You Go Girl!

You go girl
Got it going on
Strong in your essence
and standing tall in your presence
Five feet several inches
in pumps and heels
and a two piece bikini,
business suits, athletic gear
and tennis shoes
Arms full of grace
No make up on the face
Eyebrows in place
Lips perfect shape
Brown sugar
Nubian Queen
Voice of Eloquence
Hips that sway
Left to right
Toes polished
Legs with calves
that move to the flow of
the muscles in thighs
and buns and abs of steel
Perfect ten
and independent
Still waiting on Mr. Right.

<u>Marriage</u>

Me and you
Two become one
Two singles make a whole
as our desires and destinies unfold
Blending
Complementing
Friendship
Communication
Partnership
Trust
Travel
Money
Growing old
Growing together in
Business and Love
Raising a Family
To have and to hold
'Til Death do us part
I becomes We
Compromise
Recognize
Husband and Wife
Respect each other
Let me upgrade you
Adam and Eve
Soulmates
Ruth and Boaz
Opposites attract
Leave and cleave
As we achieve
Marital bliss
of this Holy Matrimony
After the ceremony
The engagement
The ring
The honeymoon

The sex
The covenant
The vows we share
Noticing others
but they don't compare
with our love
The grass ain't greener on the otherside
Forgiveness
All challenges will subside
Our true feelings we can't hide
As we are naked and not ashamed
As we wear each other's last name
Marriage
Unless it ends in
Divorce
We will live happily ever after

Good Writtens to You

I gave all I had
and now I'm sad
and blue
Because of you
and your issues
I gave all I had
and now I feel I've been had
Don't want to talk and work things out
Isn't that what friendships and relationships are all about
My heart hurts
My belly aches
and yes I cry
But they aren't tears of joy
How you play me
play with me
then throw me away like an old used toy
That's wrong and "Vengeance is mine,"
saith the Lord
Can't believe while trying to give to
make someone else's life better
I get sent a Dear John letter
Can't believe all the pain and misery
I allowed you to give to me
Alluding to why they say
Misery loves company
and be careful of the company you keep
How can two walk together except they agree?
Darkness and light don't go together
Until the light bulb comes on for you
There's nothing left for me to do
But say farewell and
Good Writtens to you.

My Claim to Fame

One day I plan to reach the stars,
Not for the fancy houses, money and cars,
But to give back to the world, what it has given to me,
To help a dying world and save the country.
So many people make it big and forget
Where they have come from.
They see people everyday struggle and they act like this is something they
have never done.
I understand it is a blessing to rise to a level of success.
But I believe it is the humble, sincere people that stand out from the rest.
It warms my heart when I see people advancing and exercising their talents,
and somehow
Finding time to reach out to others and have a life that is equally
balanced.
As I pray and ask God for my divine purpose,
I know I will reach my dream.
A lot of people believe it's like simply playing a game.
But through God all things are possible and when you hear my name,
It will simply be—MY CLAIM TO FAME!!

"LA TRAFFIC"

Necessity of Today

The necessity of today has traveled into our future.
Men, women, boys and girls
Y 2 K's, Hooked on phonic displays
Ebonics
Dreadlocks, Tie knots and Braids on top of the mind
Soon education becomes extinct
Like Afros and leather trenches
Bell Bottoms and Sodom is insane
Fads that seem to jump in and out of our lives.
I say the necessity of today has traveled into our future.
It's not just our hair
Our hair don't control our mind
And pants don't make the man
Like air
"A mind is a terrible thing to waste".
We need to take a stand
It's up to us to take off where others have left
and step into our place
A place of integrity
A place for all human beings
to participate in the necessity of today that has traveled into our future.

You Can

In effort to bless the nation and inspire inspiration
and lead to some motivation
Wanna let you know you can
Even when you have no money and everyone is acting funny
You can
When it seems you're all alone and all hope is gone
and no one picks up the phone
keep holding on
You can
When you feel you don't know what to do or say
Fall to your knees and pray.
You'll see a better day
You can
If there's haters telling you you'll never make it
Keep going
Fake it till you make it
You can
Even if there's obstacles in your way and bills you've got to hustle and pay
and don't have no food to eat and don't know where you'll lay down to
sleep
You can
If you have a baby on the way and baby daddy is gone astray
Baby mamma causing drama everyday
saying you've got child support to pay
You can
Say you got laid off
you lost your job,
Car got broke in
your house got robbed
You can
Say you've done all the wrong you can do
Tired of lying
Ready to tell the truth
You can
Say you've got your GED, Ready to get your PHD
Say you want to run a business and stop driving and drinking

You can
Say you want to get off drugs, Ready to get out the gang and find real love
You can
You want to get off the street and stop selling your body
You can
Say you want to quit running from the police, Say you want to be free
Say you want to to get from behind bars, Say you want to be a superstar
You can
Say you want to help make the world a better place
Stop the hate, racism. Stop the sexism, ignorism.
You can
Say you're going to hell
Tell them God forgives
Forgives seventy times seven
say you want to lose weight and shed waste
say you've got no time to waste and
want to reach your destiny and meet fate and enter heaven's pearly gate's
You can
Say you want to deal with real people not fake
Change your negatives to positives
and find solutions to your problems
Say you want to live good and get out the hood
You can
Say you can't
Tell them you can
Future in your hand
You can
Plan your work. Work your plan.
You can
You can have a mansion
You can be happily married
You can own the land
Money in your hand, You can make it to the promise land
You Can, You Can.

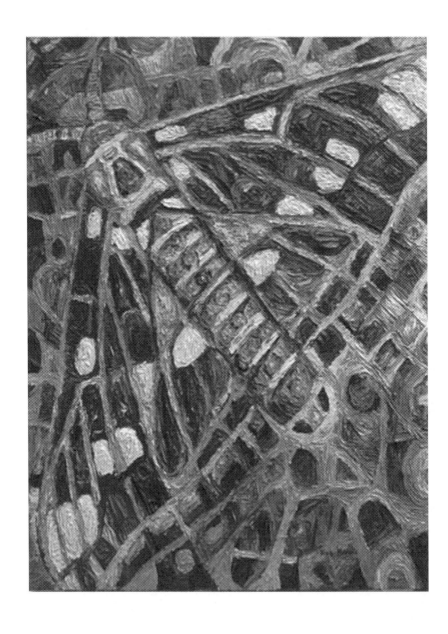

I Live to Succeed in the Air I Breathe
Featured in Rolling Out Magazine

I live to be free,
free to express me,
free to live in my own inner mystery,
free to exude my personality and elude you to my reality.
I live in a combination of emotional ups and downs.
Yet I buzz around like the baddest bee in town.
I've been let down and rejected, but I don't choose to feel neglected
when my life appears hectic.
I keep on ticking like a Rolex watch.
I keep on rising like the sun—like Maya Angelou—"Still I Rise," to the
beat of my own drum.
I've got some things to do. I LIVE TO SUCCEED IN THE AIR I
BREATHE.
"I got a lot of living to do before I die. I ain't got time to waste."—like my
boy 50 cent says and raps about.
So hear me out—
I don't need you stressing me out.
I'm stressing this blessing I'm trying to receive by how I achieve.
I LIVE TO SUCCEED IN THE AIR I BREATHE.
You may not like me.
You may hate me,
and can't stand my guts,
but I'll stand up and tell you,
I love me.
I love myself.
If God is for me, who can be against me?
If God is for me, in him I reach infinite possibilities.
If God is for me, in him I can do all things.
He gives me strength.
So on the strength though, thought I would let you know
on my way to and from the bank.
While you sit and act stank,
I'm going to leave you with something to think about and thank me.
Now you've got something to live for—
I LIVE TO SUCCEED IN THE AIR I BREATHE.

Recession Proof

I am Recession Proof
Recession is real but it's not my truth
I choose not to believe the bad news of the economy
Yet I forge ahead and face everyday in front of me
I've learned not to waste my time and money
Give love . . . the greatest gift we have for free
I've learned to set priorities, grow spiritually,
take advantage of every opportunity, and use the resources in my community
For some recession is humility, depression, and aggression
For me it's making positives out of negatives and progression while
learning valuable lessons and realizing time is of the essence
There is no time for stressing but appreciating every blessing
Divorce rates high and people for no reason die
Prices up on gas; Stock markets crash
Foreclosures on homes; Less auto loans
Food banks; More fast food
People sneeze then swine flu
Some Entrepreneurs; others going back to school
Job freezes: more diseases
Can't tell the difference between the four seasons
Sign of the times
Yet I still believe the best is yet to come
New Black President in the White House
Stimulus Packages to help everyone out
Digital downloads and social networks like
MySpace, Twitter and Facebook to keep in touch
Prayer to keep us lifted up
Touch screens, Ipads and Ipods as we sing:
Everything's on Youtube and TV
Reality shows about who knows what
Although right now seems a bit rough: Just hang tough
We've had a recession before and we've made it through
We'll get through this one too
Just tell yourself . . . Recession is real but it's not my truth
I am Recession Proof

A Tribute to the King—Gone Too Soon

Michael Joseph Jackson
August 29, 1958 - June 25, 2009

A poem dedicated to Michael Jackson and his loved ones
by Tymeka L. Coney.
I had the pleasure of placing a copy of this poem in Michael's
mother Katherine Jackson's hand and I will never forget the
smiles we exchanged on that day the summer of 2009.

A Tribute to the King—"Gone Too Soon"

If I had all the money in the world and sang in every key, played in every key,
I wouldn't have enough fit for a King.
You don't realize how much joy it would bring just to hear every song you would sing.
You did not live to just half of a century but you were the turn of a century.
You definitely "Rocked my World."
"What about your Childhood," as you touched the hearts of every boy and girl?
What about your healing as you "Healed The World?"
I felt your pain and contrary to popular belief you weren't insane.
You were a genius with an extraordinary,
Superhuman, creative brain,
and because you existed, the entire world will never be the same.
For you forced us to look at the "Man in the Mirror" whenever we searched for change.
You were just overworked and underpaid.
So today I pay homage to you.
The peace of mind and rest that you wanted,
God granted it to you.
You've set records, broke records, made hit records and yes you'll go down in history,
and be in the *Guinness Book of World Records.*
I know your death was a mystery,
But God wrote the story and he knew your purpose and who you were created to be.
You can now sit on the throne
and walk the streets paved with gold,
As we crown you with victory.
A living legend, an icon . . .
Your legacy lives on and you will always be
"Bad"... "Invincible."... "Dangerous"
I know you loved your fans whether "Black or White,"
and despite what the media wants us to believe,
You loved everyone as you told us in one of your

final interviews as you were ready to leave.
"This is your final curtain call."
We've learned so much from you, because
although you couldn't sleep,
you would not accept defeat
and although you were in pain and
the media dragged your name and fans screamed your name,
you vowed to never quit until your final breath.
Although you live on
We hate to admit we've come to recognize as you told us, "This Is It."
"We are the World"—your family, your friends and your fans.
We will always cherish the memories and "Remember the Times."
There will never be another like you—
We thank God for the gift of you
You were kind and gentle
Your laughter, your voice, your dance moves
You were a Trendsetter, A Trailblazer
You were a King—A Superstar
You were a Living Legend
You were a Wonderful Human Being, Humanitarian
You were a Musical Genius
You were "The Greatest Entertainer That Ever Lived."
You were "Gone too Soon!!"
God is love and he loved you and we did too, as we always will
because you first loved us—
We salute you in this Tribute!!!

<u>Ode to Oprah</u>

This poem is a gift to One of My Mentors from Afar—Ms.
Oprah Winfrey in celebrating your 25th Anniversary on
"The Oprah Winfrey Show."
I celebrate you for overcoming poverty and early obstacles
in life to now being one of the most wealthiest and influential
black women in the world.
Through your words and actions and each accomplishment
in every arena possible, you have shown me and taught me
that with faith—"I can do all things through Christ that
strengthens me," and "I am the master of my fate; I am the
captain of my soul."

Ode to Oprah

Ode to Oprah also known as Harpo
Who has after 25 years now decided to go and complete *The Oprah Winfrey Show.*
Since that blessed day Sept. 8, 1986
Oprah has made a difference in the lives and homes of TV viewers ever since
Oprah has been a teacher, author, actress, entrepreneur, producer, talk show host, media mogul, but most of all, a philanthropist
No one has ever given as much as she has to make others' Dreams come true
and these are some of "My Favorite Things" about Oprah that I'd like to share with you
"Orpah Gail Winfrey" born January 29, 1954, knew she had a purpose and a destiny way back in Kosciusko, Mississippi,
From growing up in Milwaukee to Tennessee, Oprah landed her first job anchoring the local news at nineteen.
She then went to Chicago, where she launched a third-rated talk show to 1st place and became
internationally syndicated and launched her own production company.
As you give everyone you encounter advice to find their purpose and passion in life
There's no coincidence that you would be noted as the "most powerful woman and influential woman in the world" by CNN and Time
and that you would have your own Oprah radio, Oprah Online,
Oprah magazine, Oprah Angel Network and now The Oprah Winfrey Network.
It's only befitting that you would be one of our first African-American female billionaires as you continue to increase your net worth
We appreciate you for The Legend's Ball and for endorsing Barack Obama— our 1st Black President
This gives proof that your name (Orpah/Oprah) is biblical, because you are indeed an angel—Heaven sent.
In 25 years, you've broken records and set records that men and women in your field would only hope to achieve
This is why although in 25 years, 2011, your talk show, you will complete, in the hearts and minds of the people, you will never leave.

Through your "Oprahfication" you have left a lasting "Oprah Effect" all over the world
Through education
you've taught us that reading is cool through your Oprah Book Club
To spreading love
to South Africa to opening up your Leadership Academy for girls
To the Oscars that you host afterwards year after year
To just watching you share in the emotions of your interviews as you shed heartfelt tears
We'll never forget your famous line in the film, "The Color Purple,"
"You told Harpo to beat me."
for your Academy Award nomination of Best Supporting Actress you'll go down in history.
We thank you for "The Color Purple" Reunion after 25 years and for keeping it running on Broadway as a Stage Play
and for the other films like "The Women of Brewster Place,"
"For Their Eyes Were Watching God," and "The Great Debaters,"
"You are Beloved!" "You are Precious!"
As you've quoted, "You wouldn't give nothing for your journey now."
I speak for everyone working on *The Oprah Winfrey Show* that make up this last season
and for everyone everywhere that you have ever touched, even when you never knew you did, for whatever reason.
Thank you for the 25 Years
and Thank you for your life,
You are an inspiration . . . .
On behalf of myself and an entire nation—We Thank God and your parents for your creation
These words only merely express my gratification
for all that you've done, for the list goes on and on
as we celebrate you in this Ode to Oprah—
I speak for everyone
infinitely as you continue to make history—
We love you Oprah Gail Winfrey
and we are with you as "We Run On To See What The End Will Be."

A Salute to Phenomenal Women

Today I salute Phenomenal Women who have come before me
To Maya Angelou, Jill Scott, Alicia Keys and Nikki Giovanni who've
inspired me with their poetry.
To Whoopi Goldberg, Sherri Shepherd and the other ladies on *The View*,
Shaun Robinson on Access Hollywood to Holly Robinson-Pete,who was
on *The Talk* too
To ladies that have had their own talk shows like Tyra Banks, Rolonda
Watts, Arthel Neville, Star Jones, Iyanla Vanzant, Della Reese, Sheryl
Underwood, Robin Roberts, Kimora Lee Simmons, Tempestt Bledsoe,
Ananda Lewis, Kim Coles, Robin Givens, Mother Love, Wendy Williams,
Gayle King, Mo'Nique and Oprah Winfrey to name a few
To having their own Network like TV One with Cathy Hughes
to OWN by Oprah Winfrey to Sheila Johnson co-founder of B E T
To Oscar Winners and Nominees Hattie McDaniel, Suzanne De Passe, Jennifer
Hudson, Taraji P. Henson, Mo'Nique, Angela Bassett and Halle Berry
To Entrepreneurs like Madam C J Walker our first millionaire
to Oprah Winfrey, one of our first billionaires
To Grammy Winners as well as Singers and Producers like Jada Pinkett-
Smith, Janet Jackson,
Mahalia Jackson, Karen Clarke Sheard, Beyonce, Missy Elliott and Queen
Latifah and all the other R&B, Gospel and Hip hop Divas
To the white house with Michelle Obama our 1st Lady
To all of the Famous ladies of Delta Sigma Theta
Ruby Dee-Davis, Suzanne Douglas, Aunjanue Ellis,
T'keyah Crystal Keymah, Keshia Knight Pulliam, Theresa Merritt,
Sheryl Lee Ralph, Cicely Tyson, Flo Anthony, Sharon Warren, Roberta Flack,
Kym Whitley, Meg Deloatch, Sara V. Finney Johnson, Mara Brock Akil,
Robi Reed, Shirley Ceasar, Judith Jamison, Natalie Cole,
Lena Horne, Aretha Franklin, Nancy Wilson, Jacque Reid, Soledad
O'Brien, Camille Cosby, Winnie Mandela
and all of my sorors of the Texas Tech University Eta Lambda Chapter
My mentors, friends, aunts, cousins, Mother, Grandmothers and Godmothers
and so many others as the list goes on and on
Today your achievements live on as I pick up the baton
and salute you in this Phenomenon by being a Phenomenal Woman.

V. FEELING

Mad Crazy

It's like I'm mad crazy
Missing mad crazy
My friend who is mad crazy
See it's crazy
Mad crazy got mad over something crazy
and now mad crazy
is mad and the situation is
Mad crazy.

Two Wrongs Don't Make a Right

Two wrongs don't make a right
so why do we argue fuss and fight?
It's like everything will be going right
Then two wrongs make our wrongs
turn left not right
You blame me
I blame you
You tame me
I tame you
Two wrongs don't make a right
But two rights do.
Why can't we just travel down the right road
and get to our destination?
Instead of obstructing traffic and each intersection
Red light, green light, yellow light
proceed with caution
Stop sign and a dead end
How did all this happen?
When trying to be just friends
If loving you is wrong,
I don't want to be right
But it's wrong to argue and fight
Remember
Two wrongs don't make either one of us right.

<u>You</u>

You could take away
the car you drive
You could take away the apartment you live in
You could take away the job that you do
You could take away the clothes that you dress up in
You could take away the outer layers of material and the mask too
You can take away the arguments
You can take away the incisive comments
You can take away the disappointments
and failed appointments
Don't take away the precious moments
the unforgettable moments
the caring moments
the truthful moments
the time shared moments
the positive moments
the respectful moments
the lasting moments and moments to come
Keep the happy moments, put away the sad
Knowing you care gives reason to be glad
when made mad—Sad but true.
Most of all . . . leave the good,
take away the bad,
But overall don't take away—YOU!

I Find Pleasure in . . . (moments)

On the couch laughing, watching TV
All of a sudden the TV watching me
Sitting in silence, pillow fights
The phone rings, quiet please
Eyes look into the windows of two souls
That have feelings only for you and me
Instantly a kiss softly on the cheek
Lips touch
Hearts beat
Bodies speak in motion
Waves to tidal waves, ocean and seas
Utters of pleasures fulfilled
Rhythms of unanticipated, synchronized, symmetry
Of anatomies connecting in disbelief
Exploring every crevice down the spine
As love handles take hold of me
Taste . . . .
Stop the elevation of music going up and down in my head
Whispers glide as love slides
From one side to the other
I need another moment that I find pleasure in . . .

I Might As Well Admit It

I might as well admit it
I love you
There's nothing I can do about it
I've tried
Tried my best to get over you
Tried my best to tell myself
I never wanted to see you
Or talk to you again
Then I see you and I
Love you all over again
I guess
I'm meant to love you forever
Even if we never ever speak again
Or remain friends
I tried to replace you
But the love
I can't seem to erase
I've even prayed about it
And somehow you've received Amazing Grace
Although I haven't lately said it to your face
No matter what we say or do
Or what life's challenges take us through
I might as well admit it
I love you.

Love

Love is like hate, it comes and goes.
Love is like a mystery, when it comes nobody knows.
It can be your best friend or even your worst enemy.
It can make you feel worth a lot or not worth a penny.
If you have never experienced it, then you don't know the feeling.
If you've ever been hurt, it is that after healing.
Love is full of understanding and patience.
Love can make you do things that often don't make sense.
Most of all, Love is with strong affection.
It should be shown with no neglection.
With love in your heart, you can't go wrong from day to day.
Lastly, this is something that will get you to that great place above.
It's that thing everyone can never get enough of.
Yes, it is that thing called Love.

Do You Think of Me?

In the day time as I think of you
Remembering all the things we used to do
Remembering all the places we've been to
Do you think of me as I think of you?
How we disagree yet agree on so many things
How when we're apart
I hear your name
And when we're together
The joy it brings
Do you think of me as I think of you?
The funny things you say
Why you act and react in certain ways
Do you think of me as I think of you?
Do you feel deep down in your heart like
You did from the start?
Do you have in mind
What I have in mind?
Would you like to spend more time?
As time goes on,
As the list goes on, and on
Do you feel alone
When you leave me alone?
How much do you care that I'm not there?
Are you aware of how many material things
and how much time we share?
Do you think of me as I think of you?
How do you feel as I allow you to express you?
Of the things you tell me—How much is true?
Questions?
Answers of I care and I love you.
Is it worth all that we go through?
Do you think of me as I think of you?

Blown Away

I'm trying hard to act like I don't miss you
I stay busy reading and on the go
To parties dancing and letting my hair down
But in the back of my mind
I'm wishing you were around
I eat meals to comfort me
When I'm not hungry
I hear cars honking horns at me
I stop at the green light
Daydreaming of you
I feel your spirit in the universe
I'm having second thoughts of you
I go to touch you
but you're not there
I want to call you
But the cover will be blown
For now I'll just blow you kisses in the wind
Until you send them back
Or come back to me again.
I'm left with nothing else to say, but the fact that
I'm Blown Away.

Is This Goodbye?

I guess this is really goodbye
I don't really understand why
Why it is over
Have you found another lover?
To say the things I said
Sleeping on my side of the bed
Please tell me it's all a lie
Is this really goodbye?
I don't understand
I won't comprehend you saying goodbye
Can we give it one more try?
I can't let this love pass me by.
Let's make this love right
So I can go to sleep at night
I'm not begging, I'm pleading
My heart is beating, bleeding
inside from the pain
Looking for my sunshine
after the rain
Please say it's not goodbye
I want to smile again
Please don't go
Don't walk out the door
Got me wanting more and more
I have no more tears to cry
Please don't say goodbye.

VI. MY HEART, SOUL AND MIND

Wondering

I was wondering why we argued
the last time we were on the phone
I was wondering if you were the only one
sitting in your home
I was wondering why without you
I feel so alone
I was wondering how the silence between us
has lasted this long
Please don't leave me wondering.

Part-Time Friends

Tell me the meaning of part-time friends
Tell me how it begins and all ends.
I thought there were associates, friends,
close friends and then one best.
Anything other than that
I can't even begin to guess.
There are boyfriends, girlfriends,
Friends that we call family.
Even friends that are enemies
that we call Frenemies.
But what does part-time friends mean?
I have heard of fair-weather friends
Those that come around when
the weather is good
Homie-lover friends,
Old friends
Those from childhood
But part-time friends—hardly understood.

Loving Me

Loving Me is . . .
It's embracing my sensitivity
Listening to me whenever I speak
Understanding my complexities
Valuing me intellectually
never neglecting me
Loving Me is . . .
Admiring my many talents
and creative abilities
Respecting my differences
that make me unique
Allowing me to express myself freely
Loving Me is . . .
Making room for my independence
as I take out some time for me
Acting accordingly and
not pressuring me or disrespecting me
Loving Me is . . .
Appreciating the selfless sacrifice
Help and compassion I give to all who are able to receive
Knowing I will achieve all I set to achieve
My word is bond not make believe
I love me and Thank God for
Creating me and letting me be
and my parents to breathe life into me
when I was conceived
As I choose free will and am free to be me
Completely, exclusively, innately, originally
Love ME—To know me is to LOVE ME, while LOVING ME!!!

It Hurts to Be With You and Without You

It hurts me to see you knowing we can't speak
It hurts me to see you because
I often get weak
I don't understand how
all of this began
I don't understand how something that started
as simple friends
would suddenly come to an abrupt end
It hurts me to be with you
when we hurt each other the way we do
You say you don't want to hurt me
I don't want to hurt you
It's best that we say goodbye
Rather than continue to put each other through the same abuse
It hurts me to be with you
yet it hurts me to be without you
What else is there to do?

I Enjoy

Singing in the shower
Positivity
Creativity
Writing Poetry
Producing
Listening to Music
Watching Movies
Making People Laugh
Acting on the Stage
Dancing in the Mirror
Reading Inspirational Books
Watching the Entertainment Channels
Tasting Mexican Food
Occasional Soul Food
Losing Weight
Getting my nails, toes, hair and eyebrows done
My hair blowing in the wind
Running by the beach in the sun
Taking Pictures
Talking to my family and friends across the miles
Playing with kids and acting like a child
Seeing people smile
The voices and energy of wisdom from the elderly and the energy of children
Accomplishing all the goals I set out to do
Making money and starting a business too
Time alone
Talking on the phone
Learning while teaching
Church and hearing good preaching
Hugs and declarations of love
All that I enjoy—Most of all
I Enjoy Life.

Incognito

Sometimes you just want to be by yourself.
Incognito
Everywhere you go you see somebody you know
Some acknowledge you as others walk by.
But it does not bother me that they don't say, "Hi."
It's all good, especially if it's a guy,
Because really I'm shy.
Incognito
I'm a people person, but I need time alone.
I don't want to socialize.
I could have stayed at home
But it is a different atmosphere
I guess that is what brought me here.
I could be sleeping right now in my bed.
I could actually live here outside without a roof over my head.
Somebody could come by and shoot me and I would end up dead.
It is all good. Thank God I am alive.
Even if I'm not starring in movies or signed by record labels like Jive.
I might want to browse around or simply window shop.
Every time I look up, here comes a cop.
Can't they do something else besides look for people to stop?
Incognito
Why is everybody always in your business?
Everywhere you go.
You already know.
Incognito.

These Men Friends

What's the deal with these men?
Trying to get in.
Don't really know where to begin.
Don't have a paper and pen.
But they say they want no girls
But real women.
Do you know where he's been?
Lying underneath all that sin.
Trying to pull me in his Lion's Den.
Asking could he possibly win.
I recommend he come again.
Is he really my friend?
Trying to get me to drink juice and indulge in gin.
Got no money to spend.
No money to lend.
But still he says he's my friend.
My heart he'll always mend.
What message do they send?
These men friends.

Affection

I want to win your affection with no rejection.
I want to win your affection and teach you a lesson.
Never to ever leave me again.
Stay by my side and never let anyone else in.
I want to win your affection and give you the protection you crave.
Just call me your love slave,
While I misbehave.
I want to win your affection cause I'm tired of being alone,
Waiting for you to ring my phone after you've left me alone.
I'm not playing games but if you are
tell me the rules.
What will it take to have total attention from you?
I want to win your affection with no rejection.

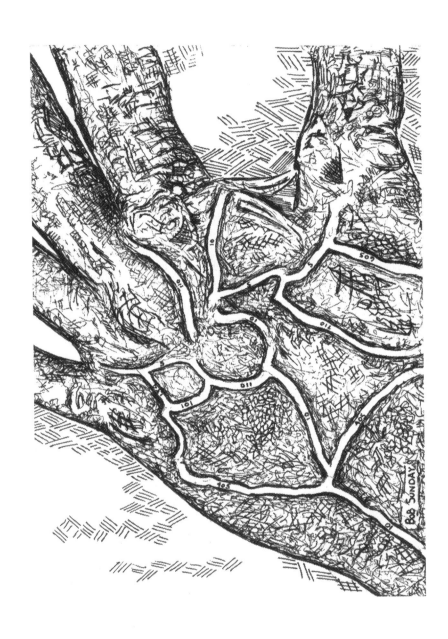

If I Could Hold Your Heart in my Hand

Sometimes I want to hold your heart in my hand.
Just so you can feel how much I understand.
Hold it to let you know that it won't break
and so you'd see that all the broken pieces of pain
would soon fade away.
If I could hold your heart in my hand
I would search deep inside for the feelings you often hide
From the words you say that sometimes you don't express
From the moments beyond your control
experienced
yet they left you in regret
Sometimes I want to hold your heart in my hand
to show you that all the walls that you've
built from years and people that left bitter memories
would prove to you that those
had absolutely nothing to do with me.
Complicated sometimes,
frustrated
but never without care.
Just trying to find a way to your heart
for me
to let you know
you can secure a place there.
I know actions speak louder than words
and words merely express the actions
I want to show you
But what do we do with your heart
until the truth is revealed to you?

Purpose-Driven Life

I was inspired by the Best-Selling book Purpose-Driven Life. It is my daily quest to lead a Purpose-Driven Life and I urge everyone to find their purpose in life and to lead a Purpose Driven-Life.

Purpose-Driven Life

I want to lead a Purpose-Driven Life
One that rids me of pain, arguing and strife.
I want to lead a Purpose-Driven Life
One that causes me to move in the right direction
And gives me the will to do right.
I want to lead a Purpose-Driven Life
One with meaning.....Like is my living in vain?
One that keeps me focused when others are insane
I want to lead a Purpose-Driven Life
One where blessings flow and windows open to pour me out
blessings
I don't have room enough to receive, while my cup runs over as I
achieve
I want to lead a Purpose-Driven Life
One of reality and spirituality and not make believe
I want to lead a Purpose-Driven Life
One that has fruit that's multiplied and a tree with fruit that's bared
One that God created for me that can not to others be compared
I want to lead a Purpose-Driven Life
Like one with the Father, Son and Holy Ghost and be close
to the 3 in 1 trinity and live a life of sacrifice, sacrificing my body
As a symbol like Christ did on the cross when he died for you and me
I want to lead a Purpose-Driven Life
As he gives me the desires of my heart as I keep my eye on the prize
And realize that all good and perfect gifts come from above, yet the
Greatest of all of these is love
As I continue to do the gifts and talents I purpose and love to do
I want to lead a Purpose-Driven Life
Pray every night and day and forgive those that know not what they do
I want to lead a Purpose-Driven Life
For without purpose and vision, I might perish when I want to live life
abundantly
I want to lead a Purpose-Driven Life
A Purpose-Driven Life is what God purposed for all to see
and a Purpose-Driven Life is what God called us to lead
and a Purpose-Driven Life gives power over the enemy
and a Purpose-Driven Life is the purpose as I write
is the purpose that drives the life for you and me!
PURPOSE-DRIVEN LIFE

In My Pursuit of Happiness

In my pursuit of happiness
I plan on reaching the top of the mountains,the highest heights.
The sky's the limit for me.
He's able to do exceedingly, abundantly, above all I can ask or think
He already promised a mansion for me.
All I have to do is believe and
with him all things are attained and possible.
I'm delighting myself, so I know he's going to give me
the desires of my heart.
In him I can do all things.
That's where my pursuit of happiness starts.
In my pursuit of happiness
I reach internally to gain externally
All that makes me happy
Discerning and learning the wisdom it takes to succeed
As a man thinketh in his heart, so is he.
Happiness is a state of mind.
It's not anything you have to search outside to find.
It's not really material things that joy to you brings.
It's not the outside forces that bring you happiness.
It's being content in whatever state or consciousness
and knowing that no matter the situation
You're still too blessed to be stressed
In my pursuit of happiness
I reach all goals, dreams and visions.
I'm writing and starring in movies and television.
I'm attaining provision—physical, spiritual, financial riches
and blowing out candles of wishes that come true.
In my pursuit of happiness
I receive all I desire in my heart from start to finish.
Whenever I'm empty God replenishes.
In my pursuit of happiness
I reach happiness infinite and set a happiness record in the Guinness
In my pursuit of happiness
I no longer pursue but I ensue success when I choose a full gift of pure bliss
In my pursuit of happiness

VII. HAIKU

Haiku

I truly love you
I hope you feel the same way
Please stay I love you

Shallow Waters Run Deep

Shallow waters run deep
as the oceans and the sea
and you never miss your water
until the well runs dry

Hump Day

Middle of the week
got to get over a hard day's work
but got a few more days to go
to get over the hump

Apples and Oranges

We different—Like apples and oranges
What part don't you get
We opposites

Reciprocity

Can you pay the money
You borrowed from me

Animosity

You make me sick you fool
Get away from me

Free to be me

I like who I am
Who cares if you don't like me
I'm free to be me

About the Author

Born and raised in Dallas, Texas, Tymeka Coney graduated from DeSoto High School in DeSoto,Texas. She holds an Associate of Applied Arts degree from K.D. Studio Actor's Conservatory in Dallas, Texas, and a Bachelor of Arts degree in Psychology/English-Dramatic Writing from Texas Tech University in Lubbock,Texas. While attending Texas Tech University, Tymeka was a DJ/On Air Radio Personality for 88.1 College Radio Station and Kiss 102.3 FM Radio Station. Tymeka was also crowned Miss Black and Gold and Most Talented for penning an original monologue in the pageant honoring the late Dr. Martin Luther King Jr.

She is a member of Delta Sigma Theta Sorority, Incorporated. She resides in Los Angeles,California, where she enjoys directing, casting, and writing poetry, songs, and comedy, as well as producing/writing television and feature film/drama screenplays. Tymeka is the Writer/Producer of the currently touring Stageplay/DVD, "The Truth," and is currently developing a music-based reality show, *The Next Hitmaker*, along with a feature film entitled,"Mahoghany Blues," and two TV sitcoms entitled, *Common Bond*, and *The Christians*.

Tymeka enjoys performing, including spoken word, stand-up comedy, modeling, rapping, stage and screen acting, and recording lyrics in the studio, as well as coordinating events and public relations. Tymeka has produced three Open-Mic Poetry/Talent Showcase events where she gave other performers a chance to share their artistry.

In her spare time, she gives back to the community by tutoring students in English, and teaching them how to read and write, and coaching acting.

Tymeka Coney's poems have been featured in two Los Angeles magazines: "I Live to Succeed in the Air I Breathe" appeared in *Rolling Out Magazine* and "I Am a Lady" was published in *Melt Magazine*.